Serenity Song:

Whole Hymns for Broken Peace

Breeze "ILifeThis" The Poet

Serenity Song: Whole Hymns For Broken Peace ©2016 Frederick
Eberhardt Jr is Breeze "ILifeThis" The Poet

Editing by: Wendy Jones

Cover Photo by: Kristen Singleton

Back Cover Photo by: Sharonda Brooks

Printed in the United States of America 2016

First Edition

Preface

One of my greatest fears is and always has been being misunderstood. It's the most frightening thing in the world to me to be looked at and not seen. Heard and not listened to or comprehended. It's been a trigger in my depression more frequently than anything else. I can distinctly remember bouts that had me confined to a bed for days at a time for something as simple as not being given the opportunity to explain. Putting holes in walls just because I was repeatedly interrupted in conversations. So how ironic is it, how hilarious is it that I have discovered my passion, my gift, my purpose, is to be understood. I have been blessed with the service of saying the things someone else can't say. People pay me to listen to me speak.

There is so much God in that.

This book will more than likely not be added to anyone's collection of literary genius. I am fine with that. There are no special effects in my writing. No form. Albeit a blessing should such occur, I did not write this book to be studied by the masses as some sort of standard.

This is freedom.

This is pain as a muse. Staring into it and drawing its description on a canvas. This is getting acquainted with the scars. Calling them by their name. Identifying the necessary of their presence. Figuring out how they got here. What I have been through. What it knowingly or unknowingly shaped me into. Why am I who/how I am today?

These are testimony. A thank you note to God for allowing parts of me to die and be reborn in the power of the word. For allowing my purpose to find me when I was defeated enough to listen.

This is breaking my broken back into one peace.

One piece at a time.

Poetry saved my life!

So thank you. For your inquiry into me. For being interested. For caring enough to understand. I hope you see yourself in these pages somewhere. I hope you see me. I have always been an open book. Thank you for reading.

Sincerely,

Breeze "I Life This" The Poet

Frederick S. Eberhardt Jr.

Thank You's

Mom and Dad-for authoring the parts of me that I see art in. As well as the parts that need major edits.

My boys, Kemari and Quinton-For the better I have become for you. For the better than me you will be because of that.

My daughter, Rai'mah Serenity-For my being my peace. I named this book after you because you are the greatest example of art and God I have ever been blessed with. If I ever loved anything as much as I love you and your brothers, I fucked it up. You are my second chance. Thank you for believing in me enough to give me that.

Douglas Powell- For being family, in every sense of the word, good and bad, beautiful and ugly, thank you for everything, but especially for your consistent presence in a world where everything leaves.

Wendy Jones-For the friend and mentor you've always been, for the punches you've never held and light you seamlessly give. And for the insurmountable faith and support you've had in this effort. The official sole editor of a piece of my heart. You helped me birth my baby. We are officially tied to each other. You ma'am, are stuck with me.

To Lorna Pickney and all apart of Tuesday Verses-This would not have been possible, because I could have easily not made it this far without the home I've found on this stage.

Anyone who has ever believed in me, encouraged me, set me straight, put me in my place, picked me up, rooted for me, seen all I was and could be. Your presence is within these pages more than you know.

Thank You!!!

Contents

Purpose

And the word says....

"God will not put more on us than we can bear"-1 Corinthians 10:13

I think about taking a dive more than often

When my circumstance is tidal wave of turmoil

Current peace not still enough to walk on

And stepping out on faith is a cement shoe stride towards no visible shore

When it's hard to not drown

When my lungs are full of salt water and open scar

Anxiety is anchoring me into deep end depression and this sinking seems endless

This life is so heavy

My faith has become too cautious to step out on itself-

Craft becoming less love, more job

Cause real jobs don't want you unless you have a real job

This is all that I have left...a hoe stroll of my soul...succumbed to pimping my poems... pawning my purpose…because stability will cost you your freedom these days…

So I'm holding on to the last bit of faith I have left...while trying to find a place that'll hire me...when jobs will tell me that my life isn't worthy of 10 dollars an hour...cause capitalism doesn't cover the value of your existence...When making a living is more important than finding the reason you are

This life is so heavy

It's the pressure of purpose

When your pen can't push past the pain

So you pull it closer just to have something to hold on to

There are no pretty words here

No Sunday best on speed dial

No go go gadget smile

Because I'm tired of giving my mask so much life it becomes a real boy

When it's time to decide to give in to the ugly inside

The hoarding of horrible in my heart

The liquor soaked liver speaking sober thought

The lungs attempt to lift this burning bush from my throat

So this cigarette is as close to peace as I know

I send smoke signals to be saved when fresh air is suffocating

You call it submitting to a vice...I call it remembering to breathe on the days when watching me kill myself is the only relevant evidence I'm alive

This life is so heavy

And He says His yoke be easy...Burden be light

But I confess... sometimes I think it's unfair that the Almighty gets to dictate how much I can press

I didn't sign up for this... this weight...the integrity of not my letting myself escape

But then there is this

The presence of purpose

A glance at the hills from which cometh my help

The unexpected phone call

When a simple "I was just checking on you" can fix everything going wrong

When "I was just praying for you" becomes the shovel you use to dig yourself out of death when everything is six feet deep and rising

When surviving becomes testimony...you become shining example of but God

This life gets so heavy

But I know I didn't stand this long to stay down

This is the persistence of purpose

When it's time to tell the ugly inside about all the beauty it's missing out on

The war cry in my tears... the fight song in my broken heart beat

The mustard seed in my muscle memory

The spirit conditioning essential in completion

The testing as an investment in the brilliance of my being

I am built to be given much

This is God calling my bluff

But I've been holding Him ace high this hold time

And I can't afford to fold

And I am all in

These are the tests in testimony

How persistence will apply pressure to the presence of purpose

And yeah, this life gets so heavy

But we were made to carry this load

It's just sometimes... I just hate being strong enough

Notes To Self

"It's so loud, inside my head, with words that I, should have said, as I drown, in my regrets, I can't take back, the words I never said"-Words I Never Said-Lupe Fiasco ft Skylar Grey

Dear Shanetta,

You were a lavender lullaby. My soul found rest in your fragrance. But we were surrounded by the stench of life, and I grew fearful that it would ruin you. Life goes for the throat, strangles out the peace. So I picked, and hid you. Barricaded you in my chaos, thought it would keep you safe. But I only disturbed the chamomile in your character. And now, I can't hear the rose in you beyond the concrete clamor we were trying to escape. Don't recognize the harmony you were, because you're so turnt up now. I have never forgiven myself. I am sorry, for making you so loud

Dear Rai'mah Serenity,

I understand the purpose in your name. See the stage presence in your smile. Hear revolutionary in your defiance. You are so much more art than artist. Baby I just want you to know, that I will be more than proud to read everything you create. From the "I am woman hear me roar" list poem, to the "I hate sharing my dad with poetry" persona piece. I am not worthy of you, but I promise, I will edit myself until Daddy is your favorite piece.

Dear Travis,

I know you wonder why your big brother hasn't seen you much since you've been gone-Well it's because I don't know which is worse, your caged innocence on my incarcerated reality. What do I tell you, that I have been homeless more times than reasonable, or how I feel as guilty as the judge that sentenced you for not being around to keep you out of there? I blame myself. I would love to come see you brother. But I'm sorry, this regret doesn't grant visitation

Dear Sons,

I have been trying to be worth your existence since you've existed. But the only example I've had on how to show you the life of a man is a walking flat line who has pulled his own plug too much to know how to live. So if you wondered why I didn't name either one of you after me, it's because I didn't want to turn your birth certificate into a suicide note.

Dear things I cannot change,

Peace

Dear penis

Love doesn't need any help, you are just fucking things up

Dear Love,

I get it; you don't love anyone, that's our job

Dear Frederick S. Eberhardt Jr.,

Relax, I promise, you are nothing like your father

Dear Reflection,

While you were out I went through your notebook and realized how cluttered you have become. I took the liberty of airing out some things. I know you're going to be upset but you need to breathe. You have been holding life bearing breath so long you're starting to turn blue in the soul. Fear stuck in your throat has you suffocating on your own growth. This is "I love you" written in Heimlich-Maneuver to stop you from choking on regret. Forgiveness is a breath away. We are just waiting on you to exhale. Love, Your Lungs

Balance

Balance:
the state of having your weight spread equally so that you do not fall
the ability to move or to remain in a position without losing control or falling
a state in which different things occur in equal or proper amounts or have an equal or proper amount of importance

I was told to find balance-Told that my desires took precedence over reality-My passion seemed to replace the importance of priority-So I asked what exactly do I seem to be neglecting-The response was simple…my kids-

Well I apologize for my lack of balance-That my situation isn't stable enough for you to lean on-This world, be a scheming field of dreams-Cheating anyone trying to play fair-And the voices that haunt your spirit don't always tell the whole secret-
Whisper, "If you build it, they will come"….leave out how they'll do everything to crowd your bases-and make you strike out on your own efforts-

Your choices, find a way to cheat the system -short cut your way in this race to the pennant and risk sliding into prison-Or settle for a d-league destiny, sandlot savior, settled with never being anything major-

I have been trying to play fair-
But a job is harder to get than drugs these days-And I'm smart enough to know that block sales only get you cell blocks-So I've been sowing the seeds I have in this barren land-My gift is the only thing growing in such desolate soil-

So I am sorry for my lack of balance-

But my daughter's stomach rumbling is an earthquake to my stillness-Child support is snatching the stand on my own from under me-But I refuse to be a dead beat while my son's' heart's still have rhythm in them-

So what is a father to do when there is nothing left for a father to do-?
Whatever the hell you can do-
So no, I don't sit on excuses and wait for a break, I go state to state and force feed you faith for the sake of putting food on my daughter's plate-

Getting cheers from an audience that gets to see me winning because they don't know the loses it took to get here-
I missed potty training to make money for pampers-
Missed baseball games to pay for my son's equipment-
The cost of living is as expensive as missing much needed hugs and kisses-

I miss my damn kids-

So please understand that it's hard carrying a mustard seed of faith in one hand, weight of this world in another, all while tight roping this tension line between failure and father-

Ask yourself, is it lack of balance, a lost sense of reality and responsibility-
Or is it trying to stand strong when your foundation is quicksand under your stance-

I am here-

More effort than excuse-
Despite the fault lines of my fortune, nothing is going to keep me from my kids-

But when no element of my life is equal

And I am constantly kept in an unstable position

Things become a bit more of a challenge

To stand with the ground crumbling around me

It's not neglect

I'm just trying to find some balance

Spitting Image

I know you hate the poems I write about you-

You know, the ones about you being the first lie I ever loved-

You know, the poems-

About you totaling my mother's face-

Wrecking my faith with your hit and run ways-

How it made me a rubbernecker in my car crash of a childhood, I kept looking back to see if you would come save me-

And now it's so hard to move on from all the damage I am-

When I am the wreck I face every day in the mirror-

I want to thank you for being around though-

Not really in my life, but maybe just in the vicinity enough for me to use as a point of reference to where I never want to be-

I have dedicated my entire life to being nothing like you but this damn DNA, carries you around like hemophilia-

Traces of you clotting my character-

I can't even bleed you out of the junior in my name-

Because of you I am a failure by default-

Do you know how hard it is to control all the things you let run wild-

Hormones-

Loyalty-

Integrity-

I just want to be a good man, but I can't even trust the people who see me as such-

Say they love me from the depths of their souls but I just get scared seeing you peeking through the blinds in their eyes-

Your reflection is haunting-Reminding me that there is no room for a good man in this body-While this body is still playing host to all of your demons-

As a child I clung to your words like they were written in red-

I'm now realizing that the closest you've ever been to the God in you-

Is leaving your children in the wilderness of this world alone for years-

Yet still somehow feel you are worthy to be praised-

There is nothing holy about this mess of a man I am-

No righteousness in being sent here to clean up all of this shit left in wake of your free will-

Do you know how hard it is trying to raise children and put down your childish ways?-

Dear Dad,

I want to say this is the last poem I write about you-

I've been meaning to give you back these excuses for a while now-

It's been so hard growing out of your hand me downs-

Holding on to hope that there is treasure somewhere under all of this dirt marked with your chromosomes-

I keep digging myself into deeper holes-

Because you weren't around to teach me how to fill (feel) anything-

Dear Stone that rolled too far away to witness my resurrection-

Dear bible I followed blindly, because all I was taught was how to believe in the love of men who I never got to see-

Dear Frederick S Eberhardt Sr.,

I do not hate you-

I just hate how you are-

How you never taught me not to be-

And now I am how you are-

You don't know how hard it's been-

To not hate myself

How To Be A Man

"When I was a child, I spoke as a child-
I behaved as a child, but when I became a man-
I put away childish things" ~ 1 Corinthians 13:11 NKJV

To my step father, Reginald Harris,
Thank you for teaching me how to become a man-
Showing me the ropes-
How to roll with the punches when up against the ropes-
Keep chin out, guard down, be open target for cheap shots, be
heavy bag for your bad days-
Because apparently when life makes a man feel unworthy of the
title-

Having boxing matches with my innocence was the quickest way
for you to feel like a champion again-

And you were king of this ring-

Man of the house- Taught me the bible with no whisper of
scripture- But never hesitated to write your word in the red of me-
Made sure you were gospel salt in the open wounds in my soul-

I remember this one time, I was sleeping, dreaming of heaven until
I was awaken by the wrath of God in your right hand-
I sat in bed, bleeding, I wept, like Jesus, you replied, Shut up
before I give you something to cry for-
The a lesson I later found in Proverbs, thank you, for teaching me
that men are slow to anger-

Black eye, bruised face and chipped tooth later you let me stay
home from school-
You brought me a honey bun-My tooth almost broke off trying to
eat it- But I figured that this was a lesson, maybe real men know
how to admit when they are wrong-

Went to school face still bruised, child services begging and

bribing me to bear all-
But all I could remember is how I'd been through this at your hands before-
Your hands, the horror-
Your hands and how my mother held holy-Like the breath during a baptism-
And no how no one ever held my hand-
How I wanted something to hold like that, decided to hold on to myself-
Clamped down into myself like a bear trap-
Held my tongue like a seizure victim-
I was a prisoner of war-
Trapped behind enemy lines-
Because rapid fire judgments from drive by looks hit too close to home-
Because though I never told, my mother called me a traitor-
See round here, snitches get stitches to their shattered spirits if somebody comes round asking too many questions-
Apparently you can't keep your broken face together long enough before our business starts falling all over the streets-

So thank you for teaching me to smile-
Through the pain-
Smile through the pain caused by smiling-
Beause real men don't show weakness-
They hide the pain in their face behind the hurt in their heart-

These lessons have shaped who I am today-
Because you train up a child in your ways, and when they get old, they will not depart from the hate-
Can't escape the damage of a broken spirit-
How long did I stay obedient to your ways-
I broke, everything-
Fought, everything-
Fight, everything-
I don't even know what the f*ck I'm fighting anymore-

In this ring, chin tucked, guard up, throwing haymakers at hugs, swinging on anything getting too close just to make up for the

times I couldn't fight back-
Cause apparently when a boy is taught how to be a man by a male
that has not grown into one himself, the boy becomes an open scar
that will never heal right-

Thank you Reggie, for showing me how to identify what never
heal right looks like-
For being such a walking hemorrhage that I could look at you and
see exactly where to apply pressure to all the bleeding I was-

See when I was a child, I spoke as a child-
Behaved as a child-
But when I became a man-
I let love stitch my scars, I let hugs hold my broken back together-
I stopped the hate and the hurt and learned how to fight for instead
of against-
I learned to put away your childish ways-
And I pray you do the same

Heart of a Fighter

To the parents of the bully at my son's school-

My Kemari is-

The eye of my twister like temper-

The still peace in my world of broken-

Kemari does not like to fight-

More protector than predator-

His little brother beats him up-

A lot-

I have watched frustration flood over the window pane of his soul-

Oh how I know-

What it feels like to not want to hurt people in a world full of hurt people-

So when he talks to me about your son's insatiable sense of entitlement to things that don't belong to him-

How your son imagines his hands are mallets pounding flesh enough to shatter spirit-

When my son's tears aren't of fear, but of confusion as to why your son won't just leave him alone-

I feel the strong urge to inform you that my son does not like to fight-

But he will whip your son's ass-

Do you know how much strength it takes to stand still when being pushed?-

Do you have any idea how much power it takes to light up a room enough to seduce the darkness?-

My son does not like to fight-

'Cause he doesn't like to hurt anyone-

This does not make him weak-

This makes him patient, observant-

My son knows your son's weak hand-

Has withstood the extent of his strength-

I'd warn your son of how hard love hits if I were you-

And Kemari has a smile like a Lennox Lewis jab-

A hug you won't see coming-

And Pacquiao power in his words-

This is a warning; my son has strict instructions, to handle the situation as a gentleman-

But he's completely encouraged to get into some gangster shit if needed-

So I implore you to pull back the reins on your young bronco before he goes bucking at the wrong cowboy-

Because we notice his hurt-

And my son could be a horse whisperer or an expert in the art of euthanasia-

You decide-

Just understand-

Bullying of any sort will no longer be tolerated-

Because despite what my son is not-

He is all heart-

And enough of that in a fight is all that he needs-

To ensure that whips your child's ass.

Love Anyway

My son Kemari loves...hard…brave…unaware of the death count in its name…his love can heal anything…conquers all…

At his mother's house…he sits on my lap…catches playful shoves from his mother…

He hops down and gives chase toward the bomb shelter that is love-

I watched him learn that there is nothing safe about love...

His mother reaches back and smacks him...the impact incinerated his innocence...like a landmine on a playground
It was a direct hit…his face…you could tell…he was too busy loving to know there was a war going on-

And I am forced to flee from the enchantment of his freedom…and be reminded of the times when I thought it was love in the air… how the explosion hit me…how the shrapnel of a broken heart rips through your beautiful

And I remember…How I loved anyway…

How I loved Brandy back into breathing…loved her into allowing herself release from the choke hold of her choices…seemed so grateful to finally have love fill her lungs...She looked at me like fresh air…But never let go of her nooses...

I remember…How I loved anyway…

How I busted Shanetta out of the city that had her dreams behind bars…but our talks of forever must've felt like confinement because she busted out of us... left me prisoner in my own home...dating other men while living with me

I remember…How I loved anyway

Toni telling me he was her aunt's boyfriend... or when my ex-wife handed me the phone so I could have a conversation with the guy I was sharing her orgasms with

I remember the times my mother's microscopic vision made it hard for her to love me with so much of her bitterness in my DNA…

I remember it all…

And how I loved anyway…

And I am scared…

What do I tell my son about love…?

I don't know how to tell him that love conquers all…when the only thing that it's constantly defeated is me

Or that love heals all…when this open wound of a heart keeps falling into salty hands and these battle scars don't know how to articulate band aid

I don't know how to save him from homicidal hands that may end up smacking the life out of his ability to love right…

All I can tell him to do…

Is Love Anyway…like it won't get you killed…like it's not only worth the scrapes and bruises but will be what stitches your spirit back together

Love Anyway…Like it has never done anything wrong…You will never be wrong loving people who don't deserve it…you will only be wrong to stop when it is so deserving of you

Love Anyway…be hero…a purple heart honor leaving no heart behind…because if you refuse to, you may one day become tear gas and tragedy…a landmine during a Sunday stroll…

What I will tell my son of love…is to love anyway…because if he's not fighting for it… then he is fighting against it… And I simply refuse to raise another war.

Super Hero

I barely watched cartoons-

Never really had a favorite avenger of justice-

I just couldn't get into the corny costumes and predictable plots-

But it wasn't their fault-

I had someone more powerful than evil penguins and fighting birds holding my attention-

In my opinion, she has more tricks up her sleeve than that damn bat belt had gadgets any day-

See I never found a cape in the closet-

Or glowing green rings on her night stand-

I'd watch moons for nights on end and never saw her image being signaled in the night sky-

But I always knew she was a super hero-

And while all the kids met and discussed the suspense of the shows they viewed-

I was busy staying glued to her-

I tuned in for most of my childhood, to the amazing adventures of her life, enthralled by her enticing persona.

I saw her walk in God's context without a God complex-

She has a heart like the Hulk-

Made miracles, nickels, dimes, and dinners stretch like Mr. Fantastic-

While being a human torch for the Lord-

And yeah she took blows, but she had a healing power Wolverine could only dream of-

She had tool boxes for hands-

Somehow she fixed everything-

Screwed in smiles-

Nailed happy into birthdays-

Hammered spirits back whole when villains like deadbeat dads shot broken promises into my innocence-

She built bridges out of roadblocks-

Crafted wisdom from the crosses she's bared-

And rods never got spared-

She beat the rough off of me to expose the beautiful diamond of a man I am today-

Mollyna Ellerbe is a super hero-

Practicing stillness-

Still diffusing the time bombs of complacent with the speed of "stop talking and do it"-

She makes "you better not tell my age" look like something younger than "say it and I'll smack fire from you"-

She's crammed in mother, student, lawyer, employee, friend, woman scorned, woman reborn, prayer warrior, nonprofit creator, grandmother, and survivor into "side eye" years and don't look a day over "I know what I'm doing" years old

And notice, even now, how she sent her telepathic power into this poem-

My mother is a superhero-

Teenage mutant ninja turtle who grew stronger with each lesson from her splinters-

With the hands of a fighter-

Smile of a mother-

Faith like a woman of God who makes mountains move on her knees-and saves my life every night before she sleeps-

There's no cape in her closet-

Just love and pride in her heart-

And a playfully sarcastic smile when she hears another one of my poems and says "baby, one day, you're going to save the world."

Open Book

(Love Reads The Foreword)

Love reads the foreword

He is flesh full of faulty pinky swears

She thinks the world is waiting for her to fix it

He promised he'd let her fix him

Together their love is a tragic trust exercise-

The story book embrace of falling into arms full of demons-

They authored a boy-

A paperback hopeless romance novel with a battered spine

Chapter 1

The mother fills the book with stories of the scars his father left her

Chapter 2

The father writes about being more than a suicide weapon

Chapter 3

They blame the other for creating such a shattered masterpiece

Chapter 4

Plot twist, the book is really a boy

The typos, scarred surface, missing pages and broken spine are really birthmarks

The boy wishes for how-to manual hands

Fixing hearts for dummies-

Was never taught to mend anything

His mom tried to repair a broken pinky promise of a dad

And ended up breaking her smile

And her marriage

And her faith

He's a great story, but the authors took up a lot space with their side of it so we never know if he fixes anything

The boy thanks you for reading, for picking up this shattered masterpiece without caution, for wanting to know more of such a promising broken.

This paperback hopeless romance novel of a boy is not finished yet

But his pages are open

And eagerly invite you to enjoy all he is

Bring a red pen, and he will drink the ink of the God of you

Elated to become created whole in the image of something you'll love cover to cover

He hopes you'll love him

He hopes you'll

Finish the book

Break Things

I tend to break things-

I always figured I was just incapable of holding anything the right way-

Always tried to handle things with care-

Until I realized people don't want to be held by someone that handles them like a *thing*-

I would offer my embrace when they would only want arm's length-

The passion in the struggle made me-

See I just want to-

If they just let me-

I tend to break things-

My idea of love is like a bald tire trying to get a grip on black ice-

The crash is inevitable-

But I still strap in-

Enjoy the ride

Or die trying

Racing towards dead end devotion until I reach the recurring collision of reality-

See the outcome of redlining love is usually an accident waiting to happen-

And I got this pile up in my chest-

Heaps of scrap metal from lead foot love-

Reckless in my wanting like, who puts a speed limit on forever anyway-

What are all these roadblocks and rest stops for-

Who wants a Sunday stroll when we can drag race away from the past-?

That is-

Until I end up stuck in traffic-

Or run red lights-

Or hit pot holes-

End up stuck on the side piece of the road-

For trying to ride till the wheels fall off-

And yeah, I tend to break things-

Have come how familiar they feel-

So I total my heart into car wrecked women-

The lemons of the lot, so beautiful outside, but under the hood there are screws loose-

Bolts not completely twisted, vital parts missing-

They'll drive off the lot, hair in the wind, head in the clouds with the thought of me-

But die on me like lemons do, as soon as they reach a destination resembling reality-

They move like the only properly functioning parts are their rear view mirrors-

So I always have to steer through their past-

They see me-

Think broken, think project, think fixer upper and maybe he'll never break down on me-

But they are never very happy with emotional wrenches-

So they screw me over-

Over screw me-

And wondering why I'm still broke and holding myself so tight-

I just don't want them to let go-

Because so many bad brakes make it hard to stop swerving into any oncoming (e) motion-

And I tend to break things-

So lie to me-

Tell me that you know what you're doing-

With that smile, glowing, like a check engine light-

Won't believe the exhaust coming from your tailpipe to mean you've been run through the streets too much-

Won't believe the gas light blinking is trying to tell me this isn't going anywhere-

But I'll believe you-

Because I need to-

I need to feel the explosive embrace of this collision-

Because opposite directions could also mean coming together and at least out of control means there is no struggle there-

Try your best love-

But please understand, like I have been forced to-

That broken things can't fix other broken things-

I know how this ends-

The crash is inevitable-

My kind of love has always been an accident just waiting to happen-

But to have it-

Love-

I tend to break things-

Especially myself

Cemeteries and Gardens

My love is beautifully horrific, like the kissing scene in a scary movie, you live for the moments...but you know pretty soon something is going to die

This movie has horrible casting-

Sometimes I'm an extra in my own love-

But-
I play myself-
Often-

In character as a person who loves hard and will bleed to keep it-

Haunted by the ambivalence of romance, can't tell if hope is half full or half less-

The Plot

There are roses with razor wire for thorns-
I play the role of a masochistic gardener who wants something beautiful so badly- That I try to save them from men with white vinegar soaked kisses and lawn mower language-

I pick them, pull them from the roots of themselves, cut myself on their distrust-

And bleed my love all over them-

Flashback

I imagine myself as a flower... worth nurturing and feeding...that someone would love and watch grow into some beautiful thing...but all I've ever known is rubbing alcohol heal and saltwater kiss-

The story is about learning how to hold a flower.
About finally finding something beautiful that won't hurt me-

About realizing that if you are too selfish to let love be itself it will hurt you-

The Present

I pick them...plant them into my bed-
I feed their earth with my kisses, and they die-
Petals wilt, soil becomes barren-
I become barren bearing the weight of losing the things I love so much, even though they hurt me-

Sometimes when they have hurt me-

I confront *myself*... staring at scarred hands trying to figure out why they look more war wound than passion mark-

I look up and ask the mirror "why don't you love me"-

The mirror smiles as if it knows that no one can save me now-

Answers..."I do love you, don't you see the scars silly...loving things hurts..."-

Remember what your love did to those beautiful roses, that was love, right?

The Plot Twist
My love is a scary movie...full of plot twists and metaphors and bad casting

I am so extra in my love...that I play myself-

Often-

A hopeless romantic with a kiss like a murder weapon-

My embrace is a crime scene-

I've just realized that I am the villain-

The serial lover who kills everything he kisses-

The flowers were a metaphor...for beautiful things I loved that have hurt me before-

That have made me this way-

I don't know how to love myself, I've accepted the bleeding and death from beautiful things-

Have been bleeding my death all over every beautiful thing that I plant into all of this dying-

And calling it love-

And I am still a gardener, that has a knack for picking the most beautiful roses for funerals

The End

The final scene-

I go to where the beautiful things I have loved are...but instead find tombstones-

I visit the twisted plots I have created ...and apologize for being such a mortician to them-

"I'm sorry"...I say..."when you love hard and wrong like me...you kill things...love is such a beautiful thing when you figure out how to not hold it like weed eater...by the time I looked up...all I seen were flowers...I didn't even recognize the graves..."-

It's crazy...you know-

How many times have we walked into gardens...just to find we've given our lives...-

To cemeteries-

Worlds Apart

I once believed that we were created into coexisting conditions…not a simple shot in the dark philosophy...or merely thrown into each other with nothing more to our meaning than a theory

This was God…love spoken into sculpture…spirits spun into one…a world whirled into perfect by His word…Made metaphor for how revolving love around each other gels everything together like gravity…and as heavy as the world can be…He let it be light…and saw that we were good…and we were so

But this doesn't feel like He has the whole us in his hands anymore…less spinning serenity more cataclysmic explosion…no intertwining intention left to keep us linked…less creation of purpose and more thrown together by the grand idea of some big bang…

This world is falling apart

Our core is hot with unrequited emotion…we don't talk anymore…the buildup of miscommunication erupting into more molten than majestic…moving mountains has become impossible without leaving pieces of ourselves as ashes in the aftermath

There is a divergence, causing shifts in our desires from day to day…rifts in our relationship have created a detachment we could never rebuild…but we try…distance deep in our eyes…I find myself trying to defend our familiar from how different you are…tell myself perfectly knit lies to remedy the reality of how good it would feel to be an island

Our conversing has become convergent…more clashing than constructing…we do not build here…no bridge binding or isthmus of interest dismissing emptiness…but we try...less fixing more friction…there are seismic symptoms of separation…we are both left shaken by our own hands…You don't trust me…because I can't trust you...You ignore me because I don't listen...warm ways become frigid…cold shoulders send shivers scaling Richter

Our nature destroyed…our natural be disaster now…tectonic tragedy under still water smiles…while we drown under the depth of our disdain…fine tooth combing every flaw in our fault lines every time we get too close to each other

I once believed that we were created in coexisting conditions…more spinning serenity than cataclysmic explosion…But this is far more God's wrath than His will…we were not hand crafted design…just jigsaw puzzles trying to force our alone in each other to fill a void…we were never together…never spun into one…just spiraling out of control…trying so hard to find stillness…we never stopped to realize…the difference between connection and collision

We were just fragments of our imagination…empty hopes of something that feels   whole…hollowed out hoping something can fill these holes…but how can you try and piece together something broken, when you don't remember what it was like to be whole in the first place

Forces of Nature

When you are a part of something majestic in purpose, it's hard not to feel huge-

And she is a mountain-

A direct manifestation of God's Imagination-

Watch Him pull the earth men walk on unnoticing, to heights those same men find thrill in trying to climb-

They make her playground-

Jungle gym-

I've watched her be valley low before-

In awe of her ability to rise from the dirt every morning and still kiss the sky for second chances-

The survivor is in her stature-

Her structure demanded something big enough to hold her-

A mustard seed mentality strong enough to move her-

A touch void of masculinity fragile enough to be torn by her sharp edges-

And I was her breeze-

Wrapped around her tightly, softly kissing her imperfections-

I danced for her, stood in stillness whenever she needed to rest her heavy into me-

She was my rock-

And I wanted nothing more than to show her I could be an aide in her ascension-

Cool the things molten and melting inside of her if she would just let go of her demons-

But when you are a part of something so majestic in purpose, the huge of you starts thinking too big of itself-

And smaller of the things around it-

As if you would ever challenge its strength when the whole time we thought it was a team effort-

The epitome of soft and strong-

Stillness and movement-

But now you won't hold me back-

Too busy toying with these men, pulling and grabbing at your attention-

Treating your majestic like mere entertainment-

Throwing shade at the trees they play with when they decide you are too much to conquer-

Whispering my flaws to pebbles of women that want to be in your position-

For the record, I never wanted your big sexy ass to feel bad about anything-

I just wanted us again-

Flowing and solid-

And too big to be surrounded by anything but God-

But I would have settled for a reason, some understanding, or some fucking closure-

Did I blow too gently, too hard, I have always had a cutting edge about me-

Did I smother you with my breath, suffocate you with air, was it my embrace when you just wanted space-

I just wanted to know why I was suddenly not enough for you-

See when you are a part of something royal that has lost itself, it won't understand when you treat it like a queen-

I am sorry-

But I can't stick around and let you suffocate the memories of you being breathtaking-

Because you've suddenly decided that the air that you used to love is too much for you now-

I've always known you as mountain-

Treated you as such-

But please don't let the smooth taste fool you-

Baby I Am Me-

Breeze-

I can redirect storms-

And I'll be damned if you're going to avalanche me into a mere ceiling fan-

Look here, I don't cry sweetheart I hurricane-

Will blow down and destroy every mention of your being-

Till the thought of us is between a rock and a hardened heart-

Our bond was larger than life-

But you started thinking me smaller without you-

Guurrrlll Naaahhh-

We are both just as awesome as when we met-

I've always known you as Queen, but I won't be played anything less than the King you know I am-

See you being big has never been an issue-

Until you started doing petty shit-

And now-

You just taking up a lot of my fucking space

Ghosts

Do you believe in ghosts?-

The spirits of the deceased still roaming the earth-

Some say due to unfinished business they have nowhere to belong-

Well, I never believed in ghosts until I watched our forever pass away in my arms-

Since then I've developed a sixth sense because you are everywhere now-

1.Your side of the bed is now an open grave...Which is to say my bedroom is now a cemetery... Your pillow a cracked and weathered headstone I place prayers and sunflowers on every morning... water them with tears every night. I have to, if it was up to you they'd just die... you always let us..things...die-

2.Your favorite color is blue... mine red... I've worn purple possibly every day since you left-

3.My life is a war zone. The sunrise shined on you to remind me of purpose, everything I'm fighting for. But now, waking every morning feels like a suicide mission. A battle without honor at the end of the road just the scars from fighting to make it out alive. A purple heart only bruised from beating itself up. I could have saved you. Made myself martyr, but you make it hard not to feel like a P.O.W. I'm always a victim to the tyranny of your perceptions, so I didn't. I saved myself, everyone says there is peace in my eyes, but this freedom has such a white flag feel to it

4.I have to move now, this city is a crime scene. I watch us die every time I walk outside the house. Flies swarm like they can smell the decaying here. I watch the traffic and how it won't slow down. Everyone cuts each other off mid thought fights on its way to the same dead end every day the places that won't let you forget that there is nothing else left.

5.I can't stay here, there's a horror movie in this skin. This body is a haunted house. You still creak in my bones. I feel you crawling in my skin, mind in a maze, you around every corner and even in death I'm still dying to know what the fuck you want from me. Why after so long of being lonely with you all of a sudden you won't let me rest in peace.

6.You always did take things out context. Maybe that's why you're still here. The unfinished business of it all. You think I have nowhere to belong now. When I said I lived for you...I'm guessing you assumed that meant I'd die without you...

Die Without You

The night you told me you were leaving

I could feel the rotting setting into my skin immediately

As I watched you walk out of the door the rigor mortis swallowed my body

I dragged this corpse of a body into the graveyard of a bedroom

Threw myself into a king size casket and fell into a six foot deep sleep

And my life flashed before my eyes

Or

I dreamed

Of the afterlife of life after you

I dreamed of that last time my breath was stolen by your kiss

Of how you held my inhale hostage

You were breathtaking

And when you walked away, you forgot to give it back

Your lips were a prison break

My breathing unlocked my lungs and escaped my chest

Rode you out of my mouth like the getaway car

I dreamed of being on my death bed with your side perfectly made

My will to live committing suicide

As I dreamed, a nightmare interrupted this rem state soap opera to tell me to stop being so dramatic

There's nothing reality about these day time TV illusions I keep auditioning for

That I have a better chance loving myself to death

That the show must go on

But I'll always write myself out of the best parts if I continue to let extras edit my script

The night you left me

I went to bed

And after the mourning

I WOKE UP!!!!

Fireproof Prayer

1.Dear God, I come before you a man... who has lost the reflection of love you made me in

I've given myself to women too pillar of salt sighted to see the savior in me

I've never judge how far these apples of my eye have rolled from Eden
Overlook their knowledge of evil
Just to indulge in a brimstone embrace

Left burning

If you are love I am now too full of fear to find you in me
Terrified of serving serpents with slithering hearts hissing
Promised Land prophecies-
Angels being so clumsy with their grace, carrying lust too heavy for their wings-
They don't float...don't walk...

Just keep falling into my life...
Tripping over their words rattling like a warning, split tongues speaking holy ground gift of gab like I won't notice how they still haven't removed their shoes-
If you are love... the greatest trick pulled has been convincing me you don't exist

2. Dear God,
She says you exist
Entered my temple with a barefoot brilliance in her smile
But how... why?
Is she a savior from these sins I keep committing against my heart
Some Holy Ghost of girlfriends past trying to Easter me a forever

Because if so you must understand that I don't know what to do with this now
My tongue is a babel of broken

So many have come to kill, steal and destroy my faith that all I have left are the ashes of myself

I have the hell in me now
Why send me an angel to hold when my embrace is an inferno
When feathers are so flammable

Everything I touch just burns now
I speak in broken spirit
Trust smells sulfuric
I can't be held tightly, for fear of boa constrictor tendencies
I've released all hope, hoarding all this hell because it's just easier
to believe in demons these days

3. Dear God,

I pray that you grant her a heat resistant heart and fireproof wings.
This hell is the only safe language I have known since losing the
taste of you on my tongue. I pray that she not be crucifixion caress
or sin in salvations clothing, that she has Corinthians 13 tattooed
on her tongue and a hug like holy water.

She wants to hold me...but all I know is the hell this leads toThe
hell I've become... I'm so scared God...I don't want burn...Her

Amen

Serenity Song

I've been known to fall easily

Lose my footing on the tight rope of love like a drunken circus act

I have dived head first into women giving me delusions of cloud nine, and crashed into the earth that I never left

Realizing they were just blowing smoke

But this time it's different

I have found the one

I'll let you all meet her in a minute, she'll be here soon

But let me tell you a bit about her

You see, we met on a blind prayer

Yeah, God hooked us up

And she's beautiful

Her skin feels like confirmation, eyes the color of destiny, the face of a mustard seed and a smile like two fish and five loaves

A body like a figure eight symbol

She told me I have infinity to hold her

God was my first thought

Love at first kick

And it feels like forever when we kick it

She's the music to my spirit our bond is rhythmic and my baby can dance too. Moves like moon walks across solar system with a shooting start sway and a big bang bounce

She talks in mantras. Says stop trying to figure things out, clarity is overrated when love has no good reason

So just let me be your explanation

I promise she is the one-

And I know I'm known to fall easily but now it's different

The lyrics of her name have reassurance in its lyrics

Rai'mah (Rhema) Serenity

Freedom song to the bondage of my situations

Knew what I needed, knew that I never get what I need

So God created her a song, she diva enough to sing herself created for me

Yeah she's definitely the one

And I know I've been known to fall easily

But God tends to make falling the best way to find your wings and I've been floating since I met her

And I can't wait for you all to meet her

She'll need no intro you'll know when you see her

She'll have a halo over her hello

A birthmark of my heart on her sleeve

She be a spitting made in God's image of a poem I never want to end

And she will look like she loves me

Will reach for me like she knows she's the answer to my prayers

She'll look like the only…..the one…in my life

And she'll give me the honor of receiving the best title in the world-

DADDY!!!!

Note To Self pt 2

Dear Fred,

And when it happens...

when someone finally fits into the broken of you...

when the heartbroken nights of alcohol and lonely can finally be appreciated for showing you all the scars...

how infected they were...

when you can thank the cleansing that comes with the sting...for the safe space it makes for the healing

And when it happens..

The healing...

do not pick the scab...

do not grimace at the growth...

do not use demons as a crutch..

don't long for the familiar of open wound…

stop being a victim long enough to be saved...

When you let yourself be saved..

Remember...

you are not yesterday...

you are not the mistakes...

that haven't been forgiven...

that you haven't forgiven yourself for....

...forgive yourself...

stop believing you deserve less...

you are not inadequate...

...undeserving...

stop trying to convince your blessing that you are a curse...

You are not a curse...

a hurricane...

destruction by nature...

it is not your nature...

you are not such a storm that you can't know rainbow...

And when it happens...

Your rainbow...

know you stung and cleansed for this…

released for this…

saved yourself for this...

find an honest mirror and say "I am not yesterday"...

"I forgive you"...

"I forgive me"...

"this rainbow is not unfamiliar"...

"it's what I look like when the mirror is honest"...

"I am not a hurricane"...

"my passion just roars louder than most"...

"my nature is not destruction"...

"things were broken when I got here"...

"I just cared so much that I stayed long enough to get blamed for it"...

When it happens Fred...

When you become today...

And she is amnesia...

A rainbow...

That lets you love her like a rainbow...

And tells you that she is a reflection of how you love...

That you are not a storm...

A hurricane...

You are her rainbow...

Believe her!!!

The Miseducation Of Words

Hearing:

the act or power of taking in sound through the ear :
the sense by which a person hears
the faculty of perceiving sounds.

If I were to scream at the top of my lungs,

I FUCKING LOVE YOU DAMN IT

What would you walk away with

The sound of anger

Or

The feel of love

If you are hearing this

It's probably too late

Perception has already misled you

Imposed its opinion of what words sound like onto your understanding

If you ask me, words don't give a fuck about hearing

They want to be felt

Want to touch you

Would rather exist in the certainty of tangible than be confined by the oppression of perception

Too often we are victims to our own ears

Like being lured in by mating calls

Sweet nothings from mouths dressed in camouflage and shotgun

Sneaking into the beauty of your nature

They speak you a prized possession, you hear cherished

Wanted

Just to become hunted, fallen into a bear trap embrace

You become as trophy as a heart gutted and hung from bedroom walls

But your heart tried to tell you

Skin screamed at how snake skin smooth the words rub it

But you didn't hear the warning signs in your spirit

This is the true power of words

The touch

The feel

When depression makes everything close to you a sandpaper squeeze

Rubbing you the wrong way until you are nothing but a walking rug burn

But then a word, from a mama, a friend, a song, a poem

Caressed you, kissed you shea butter and milk bath smooth

Held you Kente cloth close

And made you feel a million shades of worthy

The power of words is in the touch

When your soul is surrounded by empty rhetoric

Cliché comments catch you like a cliff edge catches a trust fall

You'll notice how pretty sounds don't remedy ugly resolve

But the times when you only feel good wearing your favorite lie

The words want to hold you close to your hideous and smash every mirror telling you that your masks are the only thing beautiful about you

Words want to touch you

Would rather hurt you than be misunderstood

"I tell you this because I love you"

Can sound like tough love

Like build and destroy

But the definition lies in the feeling

The difference between renovation and gentrification

Hammer to nail or wrecking ball to paradise

I promise I know

The struggle in allowing yourself to be touched when you aren't feeling yourself

My life has been riddled with the riddles that undefinable sounds make of words

Frustrated knowing you could feel my passion if you didn't hear anger

I hand over my broken and you just perceive breaking

It's so hard trying to express the want to hold someone without it sounding constricting

Am I touching you right now?

Did you feel it?

Was it gut punching or hand holding?

Either way I need you to feel it

Because I know the feeling of wanting to be touched so badly

I have savored the sensation of excuses on my skin before

Settled for the fraud of face value and found solace in the fact that things had to be real to hurt like this

And now I hardly trust anything

Question the sound of my own heartbeat because I haven't felt alive in so long

And I never want anyone to go through that

To not trust a touch but have a need to feel

To grab ahold and try to push yourself out

Of this numb...Of this reality...Of reality...Of life...Off a bridge

End up pushing a straight edge into veins or shoving your mouth into a medicine cabinet just to feel something

I just want to touch you, so you never feel alone

I didn't know I wanted to be a poet, but I always knew I wanted people to remember how I made them feel

Because people may not always remember what they heard, but they will always remember how you touched them

Hear Me Now

Sometimes I'm unsure if you hear me

I know you're listening

But it's so loud down here

And my mind is cluttered

Heart so muffled

Defeat has crowded my thoughts

Pain has my spirit muzzled

I Wish I could mute emotion

Numb my brain

I just hate hearing my feelings inside my head these days

And not hearing you answer feels like flat lined faith

I just need to talk to you

To ask you for your guidance

When no GPS can steer my soul to solitude

When the good intention of empty rhetoric has me headed in backstreets paved in lost-

Order my steps

Guide me until I'm sure

Open my heart to hear the familiar of your voice

In the lion's roar when I'm locked in this den

In the spirit of blessed vessels

In the quiet peace of green pasture prayers

I know you're there listening

I bear constant witness to the proof of your attentiveness

It's just sometimes you are on my heart when it's broken

On my mind when I can't hear myself think

And I'm wondering am I coming in clear

Coming in faith or coming in fear

Do I run for refuge or should my peace be still

See lord I need to talk to you

Ask you for your guidance

Especially today when my world's so clouded

When the rain don't promise a sunshine resolve to grow from

And winds blow wild enough to uproot

Strengthen my connection

When worry has distorted the signal

I just want to know you can hear me as I call to the hills from which cometh my help

Speaking SOS flares of prayer

Lord I'm scared

Stuck in here where it's too loud with doubt to hear

To full of pain to feel

Too much chaos to think and even the silence isn't quiet it's deafening to my ears with the possibility that maybe you don't hear me down here

I just need to talk to you

Without you I am lost

Please guide me to where I'm finally where you can find me

I just need to be sure that you can hear me way up there over all this noise

Breeze "ILifeThis" The Poet is a native of Richmond, Virginia. A spoken word artist professionally for 6 years now, the 5 time consecutive King of the South Poetry Slam Champion has done some pretty cool things this early in his career. From performing at the historic Apollo Theater in New York City to being featured on season 4 of the hit television series Lexus presents TV1 Verses and Flow. But this, Serenity Song: Whole Hymns for Broken Peace, his first official published book, is at the top of his personal `accomplishments.

12257311R00038